LIGHTNING BOLT BOOKS™

Flying Robots

Lola Schaefer

Lerner Publications • Minneapolis

Thank you, Jeff Rosen, Program Director – Engineering, Robotics, and Advanced Technologies at Georgia Institute of Technology, for your careful assistance with this book.

Lerner Publications Company
An imprint of Lerner Publishing Group, Inc.
241 First Avenue North
Minneapolis, MN 55401 USA

For reading levels and more information, look up this title at www.lernerbooks.com.

Main body text set in Billy Infant regular.
Typeface provided by SparkType.

Editor: Rebecca Higgins **Photo Editor:** Rebecca Higgins
Lerner team: Sue Marquis

Library of Congress Cataloging-in-Publication Data

Names: Schaefer, Lola M., 1950- author.
Title: Flying robots / Lola Schaefer.
Description: Minneapolis : Lerner Publications, 2021. | Series: Lightning bolt books - robotics | Includes bibliographical references and index. | Audience: Ages 6-9 | Audience: Grades 2-3 | Summary: "Robots fly overhead to find someone who's lost, spy on enemies, and create maps. In the future, these robots might fill the sky. Kids will learn how robots fly, how operators control them, and more"— Provided by publisher.
Identifiers: LCCN 2019049925 (print) | LCCN 2019049926 (ebook) | ISBN 9781541596948 (lib. bdg.) | ISBN 9781728413587 (pbk.) | ISBN 9781728400433 (eb pdf)
Subjects: LCSH: Drone aircraft—Juvenile literature.
Classification: LCC TL685.35 .S39 2021 (print) | LCC TL685.35 (ebook) | DDC 629.133/39—dc23

LC record available at https://lccn.loc.gov/2019049925
LC ebook record available at https://lccn.loc.gov/2019049926

Manufactured in the United States of America
1-47800-48240-2/4/2020

Table of Contents

Flying Robots

Flying robots, called drones, move through the air. These robots can be as large as an airplane or as small as a bee.

A drone is an Unmanned Aerial Vehicle (UAV). This means it does not have a pilot on board. Sometimes drones pilot themselves. Other times people control them.

Some drones fly by themselves.

People pilot drones from the ground. They send signals through controllers or computers. These signals tell flying robots where to go and what to do.

A kid uses a controller to pilot a drone.

Drones can do many things. They can help people in trouble. They can also be used for fun.

This illustration shows a robot attempting a rescue.

The Parts of a Drone

A drone needs power. It might use a battery or solar power to run its motors.

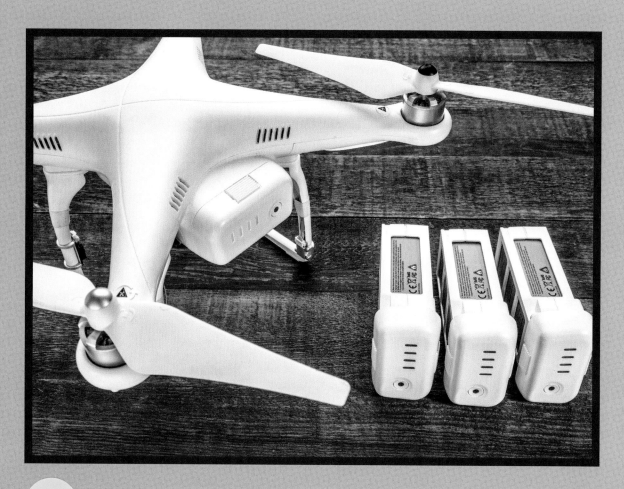

The motors spin blades or propellers. These lift the drone off the ground. Some drones can stay in one spot or fly backward.

Propellers spin fast to make a drone fly.

Most flying robots have cameras. Some only take photographs. Others also take videos. Drones can take thousands of photographs while in the air.

Drones can film while flying through the air.

Flying robots' sensors help farmers know how their plants are growing.

Flying robots have sensors. These sensors can measure and record temperature, size, shape, color, or sound. The drone sends this data to the pilot on the ground.

Rescue Drones

Some drones save lives. They find people who are lost. They drop food and supplies.

This image shows a robot carrying supplies.

Drones fly into fallen buildings or over flooded streets. Their cameras take pictures of people who are trapped. Then they send that location to a rescue team.

A drone took this picture of a flooded town.

The MQ-9 Reaper can fly for 14 hours collecting data.

Many soldiers fly drones. These flying robots find where the enemy is and send important data.

Soldiers use smaller drones to spy on the enemy. These robots record the enemy's plans and what they say.

A soldier launches a flying robot to see what's in the area.

Robots Overhead

People also use drones for fun. Drone fans come together and have races. Drones thrill and excite crowds.

Drones can explore new places. Most drones can stay in the air for three to five hours. They map new places by sending pictures, video, and location.

This illustration shows a drone exploring a new place.

A photographer used a drone to take this forest picture.

Many photographers use drones to take special photos. They get pictures from high in the air.

People are exploring all the possibilities of flying robots.

Drones help humans see new places, stay safe, and have fun. In the future, drones will do even more.

Behind the Robot

A drone pilot has a controller. The controller sends radio signals to a receiver on the drone. The drone pilot uses joysticks and buttons to steer the drone or change the speed. Some drone pilots use a computer to control the flying robot. The pilot and drone work together. Sometimes they do an important job like find a lost person. Other times, pilots and drones make light shows in the sky.

Fun Facts

- Robo-bees have thin wings that beat 120 times per second. Just like live bees, these robots spread pollen from flower to flower.

- Flying robots can travel 10 to 160 miles (16 to 257 km) per hour.

- When flying a drone, you need to be able to always see your drone. You should never fly it over people or after dark.

Glossary

controller: a machine that sends signals to a robot

data: information

location: the place or position where someone or something is

motor: a machine that uses power to make something run or work

pilot: someone who flies an aircraft

propeller: a set of blades that turn and move a vehicle through air or water

sensor: a device that can measure and record heat, size, shape, sound, or pressure

signal: a sound or image sent by radio, television, computer, or radar

solar power: power from the sun

Unmanned Aerial Vehicle (UAV): a flying robot that is controlled by a pilot on the ground

Further Reading

Golusky, Jackie. *Space Exploration Robots*. Minneapolis: Lerner Publications, 2021.

Lindeen, Mary. *Drones and Flying Robots*. Minneapolis: Lerner Publications, 2018.

NASA Drone Race: Human versus A.I. https://www.jpl.nasa.gov/video/details .php?id=1510

NASA Science 10 Things: Mars Helicopter https://solarsystem.nasa.gov/news/472/10-things -mars-helicopter/

National Geographic: Challenge: Robots https://www.nationalgeographic.org/interactive /challenge-robots/

Noll, Elizabeth. *Flying Robots*. Minneapolis: Bellwether Media, 2018.

Index

Photo Acknowledgments

Image credits: Sergii Iaremenko/Sciene Photo Library/Getty Images, p. 2; Thierry Falise/ LightRocket/Getty Images, p. 4; ©Studio One-One/Moment/Getty Images, p. 5; Roy James Shakespeare/Photodisc/Getty Images, p. 6; Colin Anderson Productions pty ltd/ DigitalVision/Getty Images, p. 7; marekuliasz/Shutterstock.com, p. 8; Malorny/Moment/ Getty Images, p. 9; Avichai Morag/Moment/Getty Images, p. 10; Jiraroj Praditcharoenkul/ Getty Images, p. 11; diyun Zhu/Moment/Getty Images, p. 12; RoschetzkyIstockPhoto/Getty Images, p. 13; High-G Productions/Stocktrek Images/Getty Images, p. 14; Stocktrek Images/ Getty Images, p. 15; byvalet/Shutterstock.com, p. 16; Colin Anderson Productions pty ltd/ DigitalVision/Getty Images, p. 17; Amith Nag Photography/Moment/Getty Images, p. 18; SDI Productions/Getty Images, p. 19; RuslanDashinsky/Getty Images, p. 23.

Cover: undefined/Getty Images.